Pictures, Postcards, Letters

Pictures, Postcards, Letters

Poems by

Lennart Lundh

Cover design by Shay Culligan:

ISBN: 978-1-950462-93-3

Kelsay Books Inc.

kelsaybooks.com

**502 S 1040 E, A119
American Fork,Utah 84003**

For those who write for those who read.

And for Izzy, some years from now.

Acknowledgments

Many of the poems in this collection were first published in the following anthologies and print/online journals. Thank you to the editors who saw value in my visions and their words, and to the readers who responded in kind.

365 Days of Poems (Writing Knights, 2015): "Three Marriages"
Ariel Chart: "We buried Daddy,' "We offloaded the squadron"
Best of 2014 (Writing Knights Press, 2014): "Night Music"
Califragile: "12 June 2016: Again We Get It Wrong"
Central Coast Poetry Shows: "My Big Brother, Winston"
Gyroscope Review: "At the cemetery," "Thanks for asking," "You remember her"
Highland Park Poetry Muses Gallery: "It's rained so hard"
Lexington Poetry Month 2016: "Footing the Bill," "Holding Off the Dawn," "My Fred to Your Ginger," "Parallel Universes," "The Woman in the Mirrors
Lexington Poetry Month 2018: "Imagine," "Looking down the road," "She lies naked"
Lexington Poetry Month 2019: "A Different Memorial Day," "A man walks into a square," "As the years passed," "I know that," "If you see," "If you take the path," "Mother's Days," "She sits," "The shops are dark," "There was a woman," "They could be bathers," "We watch TV," "Yes, I'm the woman," "You, with your hair"
LexPoMo 2019 (Accents Press, 2019): "His finger twitches"
Scare Me (Writing Knights Press, 2013): "Notes from a Costume Party"
World Healing World Peace 2020 (inner child press, 2019): "Photos Taken in Evidence on the Streets of Two Capitals"
Write Like You're Alive 2018 (Zoetic Press, 2018): "I broke a heel"

Other poetry chapbooks and collections:

Four Poems (Writing Knights Press, 2012)
Pictures of An Other Day (Writing Knights Press, 2013)
So Careless of Themselves (Writing Knights Press, 2014)
Poems Against Cancer 2014 (home-published, 2014)
Fifth April 1973 (home-published, 2014)
Poems Against Cancer 2015 (home-published, 2015)
Hitchhikers in Mississippi, 1936 (home-published, 2015)
Poems Against Cancer 2016 (home-published, 2016)
Jazz Me: Prose Poems (CreateSpace, 2016)
Love Songs and Other War Poems (Writing Knights Press, 2017)
Poems Against Cancer 2017 (home-published, 2017)
Arbor and Winepress: Selected Poems 1967-2016 (CreateSpace, 2017)
Poems Against Cancer 2018 (home-published, 2018)
Memory Care (Beautiful Blasphemy, 2018)
The Bear Whispers in the Night (Beautiful Blasphemy, 2019)
Poems Against Cancer 2019 (home-published, 2019)
The River Singing (Workhorse Writers, 2019)
The Colors of Love (Beautiful Blasphemy, 2020)
Forfeit Hopes of Heaven (Poets' Hall Press, 2020)
Poems Against Cancer 2020 (home-published, 2020)

Contents

III. From the Front

I. In a Box in a Drawer

Sister Genevieve Marie

was driving the day's hens up the rising street when I stepped out for coffee and a pastry this morning, moving them briskly toward the butcher's door to be readied for dinner at the convent. It's a treat to observe her way of keeping them together with simple gestures and a gentle voice, perhaps convincing them she's showing the way to Heaven and Immortal Life. Despite the teaching nuns and their rulers of my younger days, I'll miss her when I come back home. Her, and the old women watching life around them from balconies and windows, comparing notes in the afternoon over dark, bitter coffee accompanied by outraged rolls of their eyes and disparagingly pursed lips. Especially intriguing is Madame Tousseau, quietly rumored to have been fled from rather than widowed, a sharp-faced harridan whose happily ancient, rough-coated dog of blended ancestries is thoroughly devoted to her. Ah, the characters I'll tell you about over the years.

We strolled

the cobbled, rising streets of the old city today, its one-way alleys of bars and shops opening into unexpected squares like that grounding the sailors' church, towering gray walls broken by stained glass rosettes and replicas of ancient ships, masted and canvassed, floating in the arches, and near the top of one twisted street a truck had overturned, its load of hooped wood kegs broken, the beer flowing down the red bricks toward the harbor, the scene surrounded by tear-faced old men mourning the tragic loss.

Walked along the river

this morning as you know I'm wont to do, the tree-backed stretch between those two bridges that clog with traffic at the least excuse, strolling past lovers, cane-pole fishers, thinkers and writers and readers in no order, hopefully no one pondering final swims to hereafters on this exquisite day. A man was sleeping in one of the unused sand pits meant for evening fires before the city bosses changed their minds, aging early and looking worn in baggy coveralls and once-white t-shirt, maybe homeless from the slippers on his feet, homeless but not alone, his well-fed, watchful Alsatian curled yin-like against him to fill and complete the space.

It's rained so hard

the swale is flowing as if it were a river, causing La Llorana no little confusion. Her wail pulled me from sleep, drew me to the yard to see what was amiss. I found her in her lace: mantilla, bodice, and skirts all as virginal white as the day she grievously sinned threefold. *My children drowned here,* she replied. *May I have yours to replace them?* I assured her mine were spoken for, being mothers in their forties and living on different flood plains with men who would miss them. *And their children? I'm sure they'd serve.* In college, I pointed out, to which she stood, shrugged, and started away. *Oh, well,* I heard, *it's not much of a river, anyway.*

Yes, I'm the woman

who lives behind the doors in the hillside. It's a wee house, compared to being outside, but it suits me well enough. I've seen you under the oak that's older than everything, reading your books and watching me work. I'm shy around other people, but I learned to not hide. Can't have a greenhouse underground, can you? That would be stranger than any medicine woman's arts. And that's all I am, you see. No curses, no poisons, no poof! you're-a-toad spells. Just a healer of other folks' maladies. Almost no crazier than anyone else, except that I wear my hair a different color sometimes, so I'll have someone new to talk to.

She lies naked

on the lichened rocks, fetal in her fatigue, knees and visible shoulder bruised by missteps on the climb so far. Her soles are dirtied, her hands likely the same but obscured beneath dark strands as they pillow her head. When she wakes, her soul and body refreshed or further torn by dreams, the struggle will continue as it must. For now, the bear's chin at her neck as it guards, at least the present is secured. This alone matters.

We watch TV

with our breakfast, gameshows to avoid the sadness of the news, and she tells me I should try out for one, I know so much. She has trouble with words, swapping one for another, especially the ones you might use once a year but never twice a day. Me, I forget facts, more and more it feels, and if I seem smart it's only that I knew so much, and much remains. Still, I cry inside when she thinks I could compete on a show, sensing the feel of a shroud on my face in the knowing I don't always know my name.

Notes from a Costume Party

The Slightly Younger Brother

The Queen holds court
in a near corner of the room,
dispensing wisdom,
bon-mots and bon-bons
with equal regal calm.
Those close to the family
smile knowingly.
They recall the very private laughter
at his sister's wedding,
where he was the only single man
present, and perforce
caught the next-in-line's garter
from the bride.

The Tall Man by the Bar

He dressed as Frankenstein's monster to amuse the grandkids and,
truth be told, irritate his wife just the slightest bit. Besides, who
knows if there'll be another October's end, deep as he's wandered
into the inescapable woods of his personal winter? Unlike the
anodes and crisp, jet hairline, the creases set deep in his
gravemould-colored face and hands aren't the work of careful
makeup. And the awkward, half-limping gait? Something he's
walked with so long it's all but forgotten. Sometimes, when
somebody calls it to his attention, he's startled and bemused,
working to remember when this happened.

Caroll Spinney's Worst Nightmare

There's a man over there
in a yellow bird costume
minus the headpiece.
I heard him say
the foot-long beak
got in the way of drinking,
so he took it off
and is now making up
for lost time.

With an overflowing plate
of chicken wings and legs
on the table at his side,
he begs the cannibal question.
Or else he's Henry VIII
in his fatter days,
only with feathers.

But there's also that head
tucked up under one wing-arm,
giant eyes unblinking,
so maybe he's Anne Boleyn,
transferred to a Boschian
image of Hell on Earth.

She sits

propped against the headboard, still dressed, ankles crossed. Takes a cigarette from the pack on the nightstand, lights it without offering one to the man watching her from the room's one chair. The evening out wasn't icy, wasn't the warmest they've shared. At least not yet. She was . . . reserved. That's the word he's looking for while trying to read the tea leaves deep in her eyes. She inhales again but otherwise is still. Smoke rises through slightly parted lips, a small mushroom cloud of ending or a portent of a different climax.

We buried Daddy

this morning, but neither of us cried or really felt bad. Doris wore a simple white smock, saying his death seemed like a new chapter was starting after what he did to her since she was little, almost like being a virgin again. Me, I wore my gardening clothes, not wanting to get a good outfit dirty digging the hole in the woods, and a hole is all he got, deep with no marker, not deserving a neatly cut grave and coffin after hurting me all those nights, too. I took a few pictures of us, but maybe you'd rather I didn't send you any.

Thanks for asking

how things are going, the world's treating me, my life is. Seriously. I needed that. Not that I think the cosmos has singled me out for special attention, good or bad, Job or Solomon. It's just that, honestly, this girl is tired, but not I just need a vacation worn out, certainly not going postal with a pistol in each hand weary, never ever hanging from a rope tossed over a beam in my lake view loft exhausted. Just tired of being standing room only squeezed into a subway car twice a day every working day, one hand clutching a strap for balance, the other holding my purse like it held state secrets, wishing for a third to smack the creep with the back of his free hand on my ass into the next car. That's all. I love my life, my job, the city. It's just that one thing, ten times a week, that makes me cry at night for a private island or a cabin deep in the remotest forest. That kind of tired, thanks for asking.

Mother's Days

Well, look who's here. How have you been? Hi, Mom. We're doing okay. *How is it outside?* Not bad. Around fifty. *Oh, that's kind of cold.* Feels warmer. No wind, lots of sunshine. *Forty, you said? That's pretty cold. Have you had to cut the grass?* Low fifties. Just once; it's been raining a lot. *What have you been doing?* Nothing new. Putzing around the house. You? *Not much. Mostly sleeping. Did it take you long to get here?* We live a half-mile away. *Oh. You have a house? When did you move?* Forty years ago. *Oh. How is it outside? Cold?*

What have you been doing? I could tell her I've been to London, seen the Queen; she'd believe me before forgetting, but I haven't, so I don't. Instead, I change the subject. What did you have for lunch? *I don't remember. How is it outside?* She could be Santayana's grandchild, sitting at the small table with familiar strangers, so lost in conversation. Who can blame her, when the past is only a few minutes deep?

If you see

a shadow in the night that isn't yours, call to it. Weigh the effort and reward. The worst you can get is no answer, or a ghostly sorry, wrong house. The best would be to hear your mother's voice, your father's or a loved one claimed by time: Come to comfort in your sorrow, returned to join in your rejoicing. Speak with them a while, recall the things you still love because they did. And in the morning, seek for something left behind to reassure you didn't dream them: A scent, a picture straightened or heart traced in a spot of dust you missed, perhaps a single slice of someone's favorite rye.

I broke a heel

while walking the cobbled streets of this provincial commune James and I are vacationing in. You know how I can be, so, yes, I treated it like a crisis akin to nuclear proliferation or a flat soufflé. Happily, the woman who's our guide knew of a cobbler who worked in his house close by. His small living room was a shrine to his religion, with an ornate crucifix between milk glass-shaded sconces, common paintings of the Holy Family and the Sacre Couer above a mantel, and simple vases filled with lilies about the place in abundance. I don't l know what his moral code said of my predilections, and he gave no clues while he graciously mended my footwear, even though I'm far from butch. He was a lovely, smiling man, and my feeling is that, had we discussed the matter over coffee or brandy, we would have shared the simple truth that love is love and shoes are shoes, each a personal calling elevated high above dogma.

A deer wandered

into the church down the street after Mass this morning, when only a handful of us were in the middle pews seeking sanctuary and solace from the world's condition, a majestic twelve-point miracle moving calmly up the center aisle, halting at the foot of the stairs leading to the predella, stepping to his right and pausing as if listening before doing the same to his left, then exiting as he came in without stopping to sip from the font. I don't know if he heard God speaking, but I believe we witnessed one of His works.

If you take the path

implied by perfect lawns stretching between carefully tended hedges, you're most likely to reach a palace and all the wealthy comforts that suggests. It's not the worst of choices, having a full belly as you prepare for a dry bed. Turn around, and you'll see the woods, a dark path twisting somewhere undefined through taller trees than any fairy tale ever proposed, where there could be wolves, salivating at the thought of tender youth, or a clearing with a witch's hut and its waiting oven. Or maybe the wolves are sent to guide you to a mage's rooms, a home-school full of wonders so unlike those of a rich man's towers. It's your choice, of course, but from here, nearer the end of my days than you to the start of yours, I know which way I'd take.

Looking down the road

into the future, she said, is such a mismatched bunch of words. Looking down is staring through your fear into the past. It's rolling broken head over bloodied heels because you weren't watching where-what you were trying to reach. I have more mountains to climb after the range I'm already assaying. Those are the future. They're nowhere but up the road, path, poorly marked or fully unblazed trail.

Footing the Bill

This used to be prairie and woods, then farm fields. Now it's a suburb, though that's just a word that means *looks exactly like urban to me*. There's a cost to this, prices to pay for surveying and surviving the gray horizons. In exchange for the not-arduous task of letting dandelions grow in the back yard, I get brilliant honeybees and loud, big as a thumb joint bumblebees. The dancing monarchs and swallowtails that brighten the front like sunbeams cost maybe twenty bucks of butterfly weed and bush at the nursery, some fresh dirt, and brief daily waterings. Oh, and I got my hands dirty and my heart clean, like being a child again, or at prayer. But the biggest return on investment, if you just have to quantify, is four cups of seed a day bringing me finches and sparrows, robins and grackles, red wings and mourning dove couples, all singing with wonderous and varied voices.

At the cemetery

near sunset, though with angry clouds and sloppy, wet snow filling the air it could have been any hour, visiting her grave and fanning the memories that form the only afterlife we can count on from this vantage. Odd how some plots showed no traffic in the gray slush, while others recalled the patterns of a dozen diagrammed dances overlaid, odd and also sad to wonder if nobody cared, if it was the weather, the time, or just a slow day for the departed who might not even be there, bashful as they are when we speak, bashful or indifferent to what they left.

Each time I look

at this city, it's different. Or new. Maybe both. I find things I've never seen before, even in places I've been as often as a lush at their favorite watering hole. Worlds change, birth, decay, rebirth, a given, clichés, but watch buildings and gardens and boulevards through seasons and phases of heavens, times of day, and if you pay attention, tip your head to listen and match your voice to running currents, they can't fail to work flowing, filling evolutions on you.

I must feel at home

in this city that isn't, its veneer of bubbling color and charm covering the plywood of daily lives like those lived everywhere by everyday people. In the common shops and modest apartments, the colors fade under the smoke of getting by, chip from being struck repeatedly by the wait for the next paycheck, not to gray, not to desolation, but to less than the promise in collective dreams. That's reality, a place where I live when I'm not the tourist, flush for a week or two's stay, to the point a powder blue, glistening chrome, cherry '54 Buick headed down the *avenida* alongside open gutters is driven by very reconcilable contradictions.

Where the street splits

to run down to the harbor past yellow and whitewashed stucco or more toward the west and out of town through vine-ripe pumpkin orange, a bright house plays the role of Manhattan's Flatiron as anchor for what's to come if, Frost-like, you choose one over the other without collapsing into indecision. It serves admirably as understudy, despite its stockier, gayer appearance as a three-story pastel walk-up. If it falls sort while delivering its lines, the error truly lies in its stage name, The Blue Building's upper third being decidedly green. I promise I'll show it to you when you're down this way.

II. Wrapped in Old Ribbon

Pillow Talk

they were talking as true friends do when they trust each other with
everything about old loves and lovers about the two that left him
the hardest she asked him would you kiss those first kisses over
again and he didn't hesitate to say yeah she said you know you
could have spared yourself so much pain to which he smiled
nodded said and so much wonder she squeezed his hand

they were talking as two people do when they feel safe in their
love for each other or maybe it's secure in the love they receive
from each other he asked her do you ever miss any of them and she
didn't hesitate to say sometimes she said more than anything else I
cared enough about them that I miss knowing what happened to
them after we parted he squeezed her hand as they kissed

The sound of tides

was in my dreams of you last night, whispering, retreating and returning without contrition, a natural force with explanation but no reason, and the scent of seawater running from your hair and down the shifting beaches of your body as you rose from the waves to receive me. Later, when our skin cooled as you rolled to lie beside me, the comfort in the tides of your breathing met the safety of your wings spread across us like a blanketing shield, carrying us into dreams within rippling dreams.

A couple seated near me

today on the sidewalk of that bistro near my flat, the one where you spilled your drink, was kissing across their table, an old man and woman, older at a guess than us, clearly comfortable in their affection, in its public expression, and I pictured them doing that over the years, a private ritual exposed while their dog looked away, jealous perhaps. The cloudy day you stained your new cardigan with a cheap cabernet, after I hastily paid while you apologized to the waiter, we went to our room so you could change and spent the afternoon exploring each other, a private prelude to our own rituals, no dog or cat to be embarrassed.

Her hands delight

in butterflies, in damselflies and dragons, the barest breeze of tiny wings, tickles of smaller feet across her palms. In return for such joys delivered by the universe, she traces rainbows on each thing her fingers touch. Her lover's eyes, bare slits before her laughter, will testify to this forever, as she of his ability to summon transmutation.

His finger twitches

just enough to catch her eye through the twilight room and cigarette smoke. He could be keeping time with the band's decent cover of that song she sings him while they do dishes together before settling in for the evening. It's a sweet song, and when he joins her in the refrain their voices together sound decent, too. And then she thinks maybe he's remembering touching her there, right there, which makes her think of her body twitching in response. It's a sweet feeling, and when his body joins hers in the final verse, well, they're pretty damned decent together, too.

Standing unexpectedly

in the forest undergrowth with twigs and branches miming antlers above your cautious brown eyes, you could be taken for a white stag, an elemental force of reconciled differences, of magic and entrapping spells, mysterious enough that the wolves in these woods respect you no matter how strong the hunger you awaken, turning their heads away as I will not, held in the desire to write you of this dream, to live with you forever, feel your voice for the first time again.

You, with your hair

the color of a fox in winter, the darkened woods outside your door
alive with owls and ravens, you make the townsfolk nervous when
you come to market, talking to the cat perched on your shoulder as
you shop for herbs and roots they think will turn their sons to frogs
or their husbands to rodents, leaving me to be your one enchanted
love. Their caution is my gain.

Night Music

One: Bolero (Ravel)
moderato assai
♪=72

There
are forms
that take us
through seduction;

that
rise, pause,
fall, re-climb,
punctuated;

that
make us
yearn, unsure,
for the climax.

Two: Radar Love (Kooymans and Hay)
allegro assai
♪=198

there are forms all percussive and harsh and smoky-roomed and
there's no time for the long sweet climbing high notes take your
clothes off now I want you now just the way you want me now and
there's no time for the finer points just take me now oh my god like
an old man in a razor fight oh so good quick deep and often

My Fred to Your Ginger

One

A black ribbon held back your russet hair. You wore a pale denim blouse with navy blue buttons my fingers ached to undo, a flowered peasant skirt that floated in your passing, and tan flats over otherwise bare feet.

I have no idea what I was wearing.

Two

And oh how we danced that evening under the silver lights of the parking lot that was too hard for the softness of our growing love and in the yellow light of the hotel room that was too soft as we strolled and cha-cha-ed and rocked and two-stepped and through the not so darkness of our bed that was at last just right.

Three

Each step an offering in a different dance as we followed the other while leading the way.

Four

And in the morning, I hope we'll dance across the dawn. For now, you sleep in my arms, your breath teasing my neck while the heat of you presses where your leg crosses mine.

As the years passed

he chilled more easily, so she crocheted a throw to keep him warm in his favorite spot by the window in his office. She hated doing needle work, but there was no way she'd let somebody's loveless factory labor take care of him. He would finger it while reading at random from the piles of books on the wooden drum turned side table, at times hold a corner near his nose as if breathing deeply would capture some residue of her touch. Back from the hospital without him forever now, she stands in that white room, crying. She thinks she should straighten, a thing she denied herself when he was here. Instead, she takes the saucer and its half-cup of cold coffee, washes and dries them carefully, returns the pair to their accustomed spot by his books on his drum by his chair. Perhaps some other day, far away from now.

There was a woman

who asked him to tell her stories before the candles' snuffing, to read old poems or sing new songs meant only for her ears. He plumbed his genes for ancestral mountains and forgotten seas, his memories for the plains that spread from one to the other. Later, in the glow of their hearts and the dark of the night, she slept smiling in his arms as he kissed her three times on her forehead. Some mornings, she embellished his words with responses pictured in their wake. Now he rises from dreams of them to feel her phantom weight on their bed, hear her whisper in her sleep, and wonders what ghosts dream of.

Three Marriages

A Brief History of Art

They met in a December painting, and spent the night discussing books, wine, and each other's body. The roaches stayed in their corner and discussed the contents of an old bag. A week later the roaches received a smoke-filled eviction notice and she moved in. They worked so well as lovers that they married after a year. Six months later a girl was born. Two years brought a boy with none of the family features. Now they are less like people in love than two World War I biplanes, circling high over a painting of the south of France, waiting for an advantage. Their aim is often bad. Everything around them has screamed in flames to the ground.

Crossing New Mexico

I love you. It was early in the spring of 1968. She was terribly young and beautiful beside him in the car. They were newlyweds, on the way to San Diego and a war. Somewhere in New Mexico the sun finally came through the windows and steamed the dampness from everything. With the rain went the memory of some especially frightening wet highway, and with the sun came radio reception. The man speaking from the dashboard said Martin Luther King, Jr., had been killed. It was three days since their wedding. It was other measures of time, too: Four months from Viet Nam, a year from their first daughter, and five years from writing about that day. *I love you, too.* There was nothing else to say.

Strange Affairs

He hasn't seen her in ten years. They had a strange affair the second time they met, and as such things sometimes do it contained and created some very good things. Even after self-destructing, part of it guided their separate lives. They were younger then, often flushed with the pure joy of drifting gently on what life gave. Eventually his wife forgave him. He works for a living with machines now. The once long hair is cut short, streaked with gray and thinning. It's ten years and four children later for him, with all the attendant buyings and sellings of such events. They live on different ends of the world, in different worlds. His gentle letters to her go unanswered; sometimes he wonders if he even has the right address. For ten years, unknown to anyone else, her picture has been in his wallet. For long stretches of time even he forgets. When he remembers, carrying it makes him feel good.

You remember her

I'm sure, the woman with the spare room full of analog clocks of all sizes and ages, full of their gears knocking escapements, some running faster than the rest, no two striking the same except by accidents of differing speeds. Her life was equally chaotic, yet somehow it worked just enough that someone always loved her, reciprocated care and comfort, helped her make the bed they used as loudly as a room full of clocks. She also had one wall in the foyer, the short one across from the door, covered in keys, bright and dulled, exquisite and antique, all hanging silent and used. Her lovers knew their time with her was finished when the key that fit their heart was added to the gallery, leaving only memories immortal and intact.

Holding Off the Dawn

It's rough, she said. *For snugglers,* she told my raised eyebrow. *Summer, I mean. I mean, sometimes it's just too hot to touch skin.* But then, she sleeps too soundly to know there are many nights in even August when you can feel the temperature drop, becoming more than cool and far less than hot as a storm moves in from the northwest with a promise of pleasures for the senses carried on the breeze that's wrapped in the secret scents of rain and ozone, and if you're not lucky enough to be sharing the night, the air is colder than the laughing moon.

Punctuation

The Lovers' Moon is cut perfectly, halved as though with a fresh blade and the perfection of a clean steel edge. Even the usual vaguely hinted lines of its hidden half have disappeared. Washed by the dimmer light of the sudden switch from plural to singular possessive, the man walking with his dog in mid-night compares the precise, surgical separation of the two states with the slice of a woman's words inked in careful, skilled cursive on linen note stock: I stand to lose all. Please don't contact me again. Thank you for your consideration.

Parallel Universes

It was evening, and it was finally raining after almost two weeks of close but no cigar. A car drove by the house, wheels sibilant and splashy. I'd seen the headlights a few blocks away, but all early sound of its movement was buried beneath water marching across the pavement, making them as distant and unconnected to this world as swamp lights, or now you. I was standing on the front stoop, under the awning and out of the rain, thinking about you in your far away place. The cloud tops were outlined by continuous lightning somewhere beyond them. Later, the weatherman would tell me the clouds topped out at about fifty-five thousand feet, insurmountable for even determined travelers. I wanted to make a video of the scene to share with you later, but like when someone you're waiting to meet has their flight rerouted to Davenport because of storms, later was somewhere in another lifetime that I could only imagine.

The Woman in the Mirrors

A shooting star moves across the night sky, streaking from southwest toward west. Before it gets that far, the light is made too faint to see. This is how it seems to work: The end is complete while you're still trying to find the proper words for parting.

The breeze through the open car windows carries a foretaste of colder days and endless, frozen nights. It's okay. There has to be an end to summer sometime. And perhaps Frost and Eliot were equally, agreeably right about how the world ends.

So long to the wounded dove at the breakfast table, and the butterfly on one wing. Farewell to the yellow house with white trim and porch railings. Adieu to the sand dollars. Adios to the waves that brought them to the beach. Goodbye, Ocracoke.

I know that

movement, how you lift yourself from reading, simultaneously cock your head and close your eyes, hearing a voice you half don't want to, prompted by some chance happening on the page, or music in the background, or footsteps on the sidewalk beneath your window, someone you loved who's gone now, dead or in Boulder, maybe even moved back and living two streets over but they use a different grocery store and never go to the post office. I catch myself doing that, too.

Postcards

seem perfect for these days of visiting places I've already been, or might have been when memories were clearer. Of knocking on the hearts of people I either held in mine or saw in someone's book of photographs. Motel stationery's free, but I hate using a whole sheet of paper for a quarter or half's worth of words, and the pictures on postcards are pleasant in one way or another. I apologize for the quality of my script, but I failed handwriting in the third grade. That much I remember as true. That, and I miss you.

III. From the Front

They could be bathers

in small groups, families and couples and the occasional loner
absorbed in a book on a summer's heat-struck beach that could be
Bondi or Ipanema or la Paloma, perhaps North Avenue or Brighton,
vacationers captured from a hotel balcony in black-and-white by a
street photographer hoping for a sale to a wealthy patron of the arts,
and you wish you had the day off to join them until you look closer
at what you thought were stains or smudges and realize these folks
will never feel the sun again, never half-watch their children while
eyeing a nearby stranger's sculpted body, and understand the setting
is a street in Barcelona or Nanking or Odessa, perhaps some soon
Chicago or New York, on a day when somewhere else, some place
far away from people and bombs and guns, would have been the best
place.

The shops are dark

now, looted or not worth the effort, some windows smashed, others hidden under layers of posters and graffiti that grew as control of this last city changed with the ebb and flow of battle, the doors and walls that frame them pocked with gunfire's blemishes. Where passing feet and tires would have once brushed dust and hubbub aside as a matter of course, the sidewalk and pavement are dirty, almost silent, almost abandoned. The woman sits on a crate, holds her daughter close while eyeing a man and a boy across the way. The sound of distant gunfire ceases so suddenly it takes a moment to register that perhaps the armies have finally done it, have finally killed the last of each other everywhere, and she turns her gaze away from the two strangers, pulls her daughter even closer as she wonders fearfully if this is the end of days or an uncertain Eden.

A terrible week here

in so many ways. Our infantry, with armor for support, fought building by building towards the center of the city from three sides, forcing most of the enemy out and back to the river. While that's a good thing, oh, so many casualties, so many lives broken or ended, not just combatants but civilians, from the elderly to their grand-babies. We've dealt with the carnage, pouring all our expertise into lost limbs and gaping chests, but emotionally, I don't think any of us have a snowflake's chance of recovering. During a lull yesterday, Marie and I tried to forget, sitting on the running board of the ambulance with our needles and balls of yarn, two women like any two women, if far from home and loved ones, in a moment of peace. This morning, a sniper got Marie. I'll write again when I can speak past the tears.

Photos Taken in Evidence on the Streets
of Two Capitals

Exhibit A, October 1967

The park is crowded, but all eyes are on a woman, seventeen, still in high school, she and the flower held as offering and option in her outstretched hands already a threat to those in power, enough that men at most two or three years her senior form a line to block her yet lean away as if the flower could kill, could somehow erase their crisp, green uniforms and ill-fitting steel helmets, could beat their rifles with fixed bayonets into things of real use and value. Having placed the potent flower in a rifle's barrel, knowing it can never stop lead on its own, she steps back, gaze unfaltering, spreads her arms wide as though presenting a sister's embrace, as if preparing to welcome bullet or blade, opening her life to welcome what comes next.

Exhibit B, February 1968

These streets are emptier, a calm space in the fighting occupied by soldiers watching the scene unfolding, a man in his later thirties, an officer in flak vest and stained fatigues, with a pistol in his outstretched right hand shining beneath the hot sun, the lines drawing all eyes along the short barrel to another, barely younger man, hands bound, shirt and short pants muddied by dust and fear, who grimaces, shuts his eyes tight, leans his head away from the bullet that will arrive by the time the next, post mortem frame is taken and he sprawls gracelessly on concrete. Having carried out the sentence, the first man holsters his pistol, turns, and moves on to the next act of war.

Sidewalk Requiem

plays on the radio, leaving no choice but to think about that evening when Bobby lay dying up in Los Angeles along with so many dreams, the weighted tears she and I both cried, the choice we danced around. So soon after King's death in early April, so close to my ship's deployment to the coast near Danang, I felt ripped apart, was ready to pack the few things we owned and drive north, cross out of this self-destructing land into Canada and asylum at the Peace Arch. She wanted the child she carried to be born in America. So we stayed. And here we are, fifty years later, more on the same page now, both wondering if it's time at last to take that drive, to cry uncle as a rational response to a nation's rush to murder-suicide.

Imagine

the party: All your big brother's friends from high school. The neighbors. Some favorite teachers, even Mrs. Miller from third grade of all people. Local family, an uncle from up in Milwaukee who was more like a brother to both of you. His girlfriends from over the years all in one place and being kind to each other. Your dad was proud to have a son going off to war, since he hadn't been able to as much as he tried, stuck his four years behind a desk on the safe side of the ocean. It always galled him to have to admit he never fought.

the letter: I was watching our asses while Gunny showed some of the Fuckin' New Guys how to dig out a beer can mine the Bad Guys left behind on the edge of the road. Turned out there was a bigger, pressure-triggered mine underneath it. Somehow all the shrapnel missed me. I flew out to the hospital ship holding the bloody hand of an eighteen-year old kid who kept screaming until the morphine set in or he bled out. I'm not sure which. Padre Jacobs from the ship gave him Last Rites on the flight deck, and we carried him down to the morgue. So tell me, Dad. Please. What do you think you missed, and what do you think about this wonderful war of yours now?

the photo: Low, simple buildings line a dirt street. A shadowed body leans out a doorway. The muzzle of a rifle and the camera lens stare into each other. It's the last image on your big brother's camera.

the flag-draped coffin: Imagine.

The country

here is amazing in its possibly infinite beauty. The Delta and karst, forests and jungles. Marble Mountain and China Beach. Even the riotous, strutting cities and the rice-paddied, struggling villages. Except the parts we've bombed and burned the shit out of and pissed on with misty Orange Crush. Even Bosch could see nothing to admire in them, what our sick alchemy has wrought. And the people are lovely, welcoming, the children like children everywhere, though I guess we'd be nice to armed strangers roaming our country at will, hoping they'd reciprocate while fearing the worst, praying the next generation would be spared.

We offloaded the squadron

to the airfield at Phu Bai two weeks ago, the February weather hot and steamy, making the air just above the flight deck shimmer. Working on the gun radar on top of Three was like being a pancake on a griddle, but at least there was shade along the catwalk when I started to gray out; watches sitting in the director tub atop the island were just plain brutal, even after sunset. In the Midwest, we would have said the air was very close.

A week ago we made Yokosuka near sundown, and woke in the morning to five inches of fresh snow on the flight deck and the heating system on the fritz. If I couldn't take enough clothes off to be comfortable that last day off Nam, after nine months in coastal waters I couldn't wear enough to ward the cold while working and standing watch, even below decks. Looking forward to being with you again, but not looking forward to readapting to four seasons.

And now we're headed for Pearl, passing through the tail of a typhoon that's probably a relative of the one that chased us out of Okinawa last July. Even the Old Man is seasick today, and there's white water across the flight deck as we roll and pitch more than riders at an amusement park. Working around the urge to barf, it's taken me two hours to write this. Enough said. How's the weather there in Chicago?

My Big Brother, Winston

one

The role of government is to take away *no*, leaving masses in the
streets to chant, *More war! More war!;* leaving women to kneel
and say *yes* regardless of their hearts; freeing lovers and children
and friends to call the police at will.

The writer's job is current truth, which later the editor redacts, the
historian improves by deletion, and the fireman washes in flame:
All of these bathed in sound logic, toweled dry with rough terry
and kissed on the cheek, before slouching off to their dreams.

two

Boats are burning on the water,
reflecting the firelight of cities.
This is not the way it was,
though I've pretended to forget:

One uncle fighting in Korea,
sole survivor in his unit.
The other serving near Saigon
in the days before it all fell down.

Not knowing if November would come
and find us in our daily lives,
or October would mark the end
of us and our pretended genius.

Hiding under school desks,
as if they'd shield from radiation
gifted us by the horrid Russians.
MAD, the perfect final acronym.

They were the enemy.
We were the good guys.
Truth was something we knew.
And now we risk dying in one boat.

three

Which comes first: The witch, or the need to hunt her? Her
warlock, even in that title, threatens equally, gives cause for
protective, quick destruction. You can help stop them. Must. They
might come for you next, may weave you in their lies. I hope
you're joking, foolishly, when you ask which *they* I mean.

Love is dangerous, you know, friendship ever suspect. Truth is
Janus-faced, fluid. We'll need to take that magazine; there are
revisions to an article. Is that a book under your pillow? Perhaps
you have a lighter. No? Then allow me the deep pleasure, it's
orgasmic grimace hidden behind the Janus-mask of Duty.

The year and place overlap fully, the temperature and globe as
well. You are here. Wherever you are is here: Present and Future.
Past, unless you believe your memories more than what I tell you
is best. One man's dystopia, another's heaven made flesh and
blood. The labels scrawled in bold blocks on this Venn diagram
don't matter.

You are here.

four

Passing in the street: *Can I see you?*
Later in the day: *Yes. Tomorrow night.*
As unnoticed as two high-schoolers
in the noise of a crowded hall,
or two grown lovers in a dangerous time
trying every way they can find to survive
until the next sharing of small deaths.

And even those will be whispered,
no more or less than endearments,
or their laughter, or joy, sadness:
The things they would shout,
as totally subversive as cheating spouses,
these two cuckolders of the State
in their game of orgasmic roulette.

Not the first. Not the last to come,
even as it holds their personal ends.
This simple, impossible coup d'amour
with no beginning and no end,
no chance of making any matter.
Standing in a crowd: *Seen Julia?*
A day or two later: *No. Winston?*

five

My freshly minted ghost met yours in amber sunlight on the browned field where our bodies became lovers before our souls. *I betrayed you,* you said, *told them every detail of our insurrectionists' affair. And blamed you for it all.* As if I hadn't done the same, speaking through pain like some untried teen-aged poet going on about the most common events. I even begged and hoped for you to suffer. But that was not my real burden. Even as our ghosts parted, sunset fading as the snow began, I enacted my betrayal once again: I didn't say that I still love you.

A man walks into a square

and almost endless expanse of concrete, stops in the path of a tank, and waves his arms. Confronted with his pants and shirt, black and white cloth simple against the gray landscape, the green and brown of the metal beast's skin seem almost festive. One day, perhaps, there will be celebrations here, but now only the silence of a world's held breaths and a world's stilled hearts, waiting, afraid to look, afraid to look away. So many endings stretch toward the horizon, so many ways for one man to live or die protesting yesterday's uncounted deaths in this same place, but in the end we choose the easiest: A man walks out of a square, and is forgotten.

The crosses at Arlington

this afternoon only seemed to go on forever, blending in my mind's eye with the fields of other military cemeteries I've walked, the many seen in photographs and films across the years. They roll on in my memory now like ocean whitecaps seen by a child from eight thousand feet above, or from the signal bridge of a small carrier in mid-ocean ten years later, or perhaps a forest of intentional beech trees towering in their quest for Heaven seen from the center still later, the difference being the crosses should never have happened.

12 June 2016: Again We Get It Wrong

Yesterday's heat has given way to moderation, and I'm out front, down on my old, stiff hands and thick, aching knees, tending the varied wealth of our flower beds. Last year's rose of Sharon volunteers need cleaning out, before they root so deep I'll need a spade and back brace. Or maybe dynamite. There are days I'm almost frustrated enough to blow the place up and down and start over. Don't worry. Ain't gonna' happen. I know better than to do that. But I swear this process will take forever. Meanwhile, it's five days before the first anniversary of Charleston, and down in Orlando the clean-up crews aren't even starting to get ready. The crime scene will take a week of forevers to process. A score dead, two score wounded, somebody with a score to settle. When they get fed up enough with whatever they're personally, self-righteously fed up with, some folks just want the sound of gunfire to start over, to raise their spirits up and strike the others down. Why does the wrongness of this take forever for us to process?

A Different Memorial Day

one

Remembering the safari films the local pharmacist would show to various groups on Friday nights: I turn away before the shot comes. When they are gone, when in our greed we've killed them all, what will we kill next? What happens when we come to us, alone but for livestock and pets?

two

How does any parent, even in anger at their partner, accidentally beat a four-year old girl to death? How does anyone dump that body, entombed by a black garbage bag, in a rural roadside ditch?

three

If you don't take your own life before the police bring you down, please tell me how the eight people you just shot caused you to lose your job, your house, your spouse and children, a bet, a fight, your temper, your humanity.

four

Argue as you will the merits of war. Of self-defense. Of a hierarchy of evil. Tell me of blind rage and insanity. I'll grant you every foolish reason, just to clear the smoke from the field.

Now, stick to the question: In our daily lives, how do we come to this?

Down the rabbit hole

online this afternoon, watching a video of Yevtushenko's Babi Yar
set to music, holding back tears, cries, retch. After, scrolling down
past atrocity after atrocity, all committed against the Other by men
who believed their acts were justified and necessary to honor
Country and Leader, and in the middle of these, at once as normal
yet bizarrely sited as a Sunday picnic in a forest preserve,
Madonna's Material Girl.

There was a die-in

downtown today, a couple hundred students from the university lying crumpled on the street for a full block to speak without words against the violence encroaching deeper each day into the landscape of life, and the evening news said more about the inconvenience caused. I thought of a remote taxi-way at the airport filled with the supposedly injured and dying, all in rough make-up as part of a crash drill for surrounding EMS, ambulances and fire trucks everywhere, and how the airlines didn't want arriving passengers scared by thinking it could be real. Which led me, fifty years after, to the carnage on the flight deck when they flew in six medevac birds, all loaded, the real blood from real wounds bathing real bodies, the efforts at triage and the clergy trying to at least save souls, how it never made the news at all until just now.

About the Author

Lennart Lundh is a poet, historian, photographer and short-fictionist. His work has appeared internationally since 1965, including poetry in some forty anthologies and numerous issues of more than seventy-five journals. Len served in Vietnam with the Navy's Amphibious Ready Group Bravo during 1968 and 1969, and was honorably discharged as a conscientious objector in 1970. He and his high school sweetheart are great-grandparents, and reside in Northeastern Illinois.